LIFE IN AN AQUARIUM

poems

LIFE IN AN AQUARIUM

poems

TRIJIT MUKHERJEE

Hawakal
PUBLISHERS
New Delhi | Calcutta

HAWAKAL PUBLISHERS PRIVATE LIMITED
70 B/9 Amritpuri, East of Kailash, New Delhi 65
33/1/2 K B Sarani, Mall Road, Calcutta 80

Email info@hawakal.com
Website www.hawakal.com

Cover designed by Bitan Chakraborty

First edition (paperback) July 2022

ISBN: 978-93-91431-01-3 (paperback)

Price: INR 150 | USD 11.99

for
my parents

FOREWORD

Trijit Mukherjee's poems speak of the reality of life that unfolds in front of young eyes that have been seeing the world through a poetic lens. While a poem like "Sleeping Under the Stars" does bring in an element of romanticism — "I was lying on the field near the river/ No pillows, just the verdant grasses" another poem "Streetlight" voices the harsh reality of life for the myriad whose life is a story of struggle at each step — "You have no abode, no kinsman, no allies/ The sidewalk is your only trace."

The young voice speaks of pain, suffering, and angst, yet the lines bring faint hints of hope that sometimes struggles to shine through. Using an idiom that is simple and jarred in keeping with the emotions voiced, the poems have images from the mundane world, which blend in thought and feeling.

Mukherjee is a poet whom I have seen and read over the past two years. The early poems have now led on to a more mature voice that in the coming days will be honed even further. I would recommend him as a young poetic voice that needs to be heard.

NISHI PULUGURTHA
June 2022
Calcutta

Contents

SLEEPING UNDER STARS

One day after another goes away.
Many fond memories pass away.
The breeze blows far and wide.
The seasons are changing years after years.
I was lying on the field near the river.
No pillows, just the verdant grasses.
The sour sound of crickets was coming from aside.
Since there was no sleep in my eyes,
I gazed at the stars, they were glittering,
tried a bit of conjecture what they meant.
They were continuously flickering and flickering.
We do not have the time to think about stars.
Usually they do not make a minute to think.
They too want to tell many unknown tales.
I want to hear them all, time is shorting everyday
However, it's dawn.

STREETLIGHT

You were born on the sidewalk.
There was none with you, but your greatest hero.
You have no abode, no kinsman, no allies.
The sidewalk is your only trace.
Your dad still has to pull the rickshaw.
Surviving is the only object,
that street water tap is the beacon to stay alive.
To live on the footpath is more dangerous than trouble,
whether the monster truck or another four-wheelers,
saving yourself from those will be the only goal then.
If the hard time passes,
if the alternative era comes,
if you survive on this footpath,
you will rise,
in a new way, by the new light, on the new day.
If you got bemused, are unable to find an answer,
look at that streetlight, that's still on.
That will give you a hope, silent hope,
that will tell you about your struggle.
And your days are coming.

HEAVEN SENT

Didn't you commit the sin in your last birth?
Whether stealthily or deliberately, sin is sin.
Sin must be atoned, even before death.
"To err is human"
Are all mistakes forgiven?
This is your new birth, the metempsychosis.
Remember the journey of your previous birth?
You've been suffered by the basilisk smoke of the abyss,
your demise did not go well.
Unexpectedly in this birth, you came from heaven.
Your soul is purified like an infant.
Life is still left, like a white page.
Don't commit a sin, come out of hades,
no more dust, no more mud-slinging.
You can adequate yourself in this time.
Heaven will open the gate for you.

EDGE OF 2061

Pal, what's been going on?
How much you are smiling at the end of the day?
Haven't heard from you for a long time.
You moved to Yorkshire, started your new life.
Since childhood, we were best of buddies.
You always like to write stories.
Those were not the days when I'd not chat with you.
We were tagging each other on social media.
How many years have been passed through!
Nowadays, social media is running faster,
I got many friends on Facebook, so many loves.
You are missing among them.
I lost many friends in last few years,
there is no way left to contact them.
I retired a week ago from my job.
But...
On 2040, someone confirmed me about your death.
I tried to contact your family, I wasn't able to.
I have lot of a time now, still cannot hear you
I'll remember you, I'll sit again next to you,
in our next birth, in the same school, on the same bench.

TOSS THE COIN

Why do we toss coins?
Just for the sport matches or to know about our fate?
The vice versa of a coin, always paralleled.
People are still following superstitions,
they think a coin is like a lottery ticket.
We buy them and examine our fate.
Most of the time we fail.
Some thought coins are the key to their destiny!
If you toss your coin, will poverty go away?
Can you win a match by just winning the toss?
A coin belongs to both, head and tail.
But time only stays on one side,
who turns around and rises.
Despite winning tosses, some lost their matches.
Sometimes after winning the tickets,
all problem won't be sorted.
None knows the result prior.
Yet the thought of sore between winning and losing,
Worries you a lot. Doesn't it?

LIFE IN AN AQUARIUM

This human life of ours, is an unique one.
We like to feed dogs, tie them by chain,
or to keep birds in a cage, fishes in an aquarium.
We do this all for our whims of mind.
Our lives are too confined in an aquarium.
Neither chains around our neck, nor cages outside,
the thick glass is missing too, still have something.
We cannot go beyond that, even if we want to.
Like fishes, our lives are easeful and felicitous.
Life is full of internet, reverie and genius.
Ignoring superstitions, keeping Science as a witness,
and with God's blessings, this life is going on.
Green trees, brown deserts, deep oceans, snow-capped hills,
and the busy life are surrounding this world.
The magnificent sky keeps an eye on us.
You may say this is our trivial life.
None cares for each other, that concealed the globe outside.
This is our life, in an Aquarium.

LITTLE LAUGHS ARE NEVER BAD

Losing an argument with your man,
to lose one's purpose or to lose intentionally,
or to lose to your destiny by punishing an innocent.
There is no branch or branches to lose,
losing is called losing.
The problem is always between victory and defeat.
Someone gets pleasure by seeing other's defeat,
someone finds joy in winning over others,
while others lose themselves.
Some seek happiness by ruining others,
while others seek happiness by completing themselves.
In the midst of joy, there is sorrow of losing.
Some admit their defeat and walk away from the path,
some are grinned and said goodbyes.
A smirk on the lips while saying goodbye is never bad.
Perhaps it's the last laugh of the last day,
or an indication of something big on the big day,
where you and I are, none knows.

UFF... THIS HOMEWORK

I went to school after a long time today,
don't know why all are weeping;
none knows anyone, all are unknown.
Abruptly a stranger kept his hand on my shoulder,
said about the homework!
That school, I never wanted to go.
Parents forcibly used to send me there,
the teachers seemed so angry,
burden of my bag, the subjects were horrible,
the fun with allies while returning home was best.
The teachers were giving us the homework everyday,
Grammars and Algebras were like complicated;
the formulas were too tough to memorize.
It'd seem better to leave the school as soon as possible.
Today, standing at the door of class twelve,
coming here to take my higher-secondary marksheet.
I've no answer.
Time and desire are giving me answers.
Nothing left to go back to the same classes.
Dust is gathering in the gaps of mind, no duster needed.
Perhaps, I would get a homework again.
Perhaps, the homework to be a good human being.

THE LACHRYMAL SOCIETY

Toxic, the society is poisoned by curse.
Nothing left to describe the poisonous effect.
Seven sins have been mixed up.
The feeling is getting lost,
no more taste in the mouth,
sadness is in the sacred mind.
I gave up trying, that empty field.
Dew honey seems tasteless,
still a fake smile exist.
What if the back touches the wall?
Nothing to lose now.
none keeps their hand on the shoulder and assures us.
Then we see the end of the world,
good thought and oxygen are poisoned.
Poison is weaving a net between good and evil.
What else can be good?
The yard submerged in the sea,
Venomous fungus or cactus, a city in the rain of pain.
White sheet turns red by bad blood,
death, mutilated bodies and pavements are just an excuse.
The big people are laughing in the dark,
broken chairs, dusty glasses and an Amnesia,
go away, don't ever come back.

THE LAST FLIGHT

The fastest thing in our cosmos is time,
faster than the reverie of the fictitious universe.
We think a lot, but everything is measurable.
None will get out of it,
whether it's a busy life in New York,
or someone's desire to get more pain,
or pray to God for someone, to be together, forever.
It can be cursed at any time.
Ashes of woe are floating in the dead wind,
discerning your back against the wall before the disaster,
if the friendship breaks you down, think about it.
We create that in our imagination only,
when it will not be in reality.
We are born knowing that one day we will die,
just some undone works, some leftover desires,
yet something remains good.
Even if we could have been better all the time,
the epitaphs didn't have to take place in such a terrible way.

DIM, DIM, SWALLOW

You woke up in middle of the night of psychedelic,
he got some words to justify your autotelic.
Sometimes it's like someone took a knife,
you don't want to see yourself as your strife.
He threw a knife through the middle of your skull,
timber, o mine, they got their safety and a stull.
You got a bad desire, with lots of harm and blood,
he sowed broken bones beside a rodent flood.
Polypeptides are several with that reversible Chalone,
did he go away and leave you all alone?
The city of full violence with some brutal spies,
disgusting and offences are filled up with your vice.
You are a victim, with having a dim,
if you open your eyes you must see his grim.
With the neighing of a white horse,
his neck bleeds causes of a gorse.
Blood is oozing from the ice,
Omega, through him, will take you for a trice.

DIRE PERIL

The day started with a noteless fact,
do not know what will be the another worse impact.
Do not know if it is bad to be optimistic,
or I have to wear mask to be a socialistic!
Losing you at empty night,
or getting involved into a fistfight.
The writer is using dramaturgy,
words establish him as a playwright.
We can live in fear,
if we hear something worse about our dear.
To me, you always being a taciturn,
rapidly I wish your return.
How many days I shall detain?
in my every cantos of mine, I want you to retain.
People are transient with their desire,
me like a vagient writing a satire.
Everyone somewhere using tools like tumbril,
to keep someone living in dire peril.

HE, AN INAMORATO

The sleep in eyes,
the dew drops are only you.
The thirst of lips,
the hope to live is only you.
The blurred shadows on my thought,
the morning rain is you,
a little of me, a little of you,
lost in love.
I wake up in my sleep for you,
why every happiness smiles only for you?
I am your face, you are my mirror,
come erase all distances,
a little of me, a little of you,
didn't fall apart.
Why do you talk about me in my thoughts?
Why do you live like this in my question?
Your perfume smells so good,
like a fresh red rose.
I wish you were mine, you stay mine,
turn on the light, remove the darkness,
a little of me, a little of you
lost in love,
a little of me, a little of you,
didn't fall apart.

WHERE IS MY MIND?

And I begin to find my mind,
I never expected you as mine.
And I am writing about you,
I like the eerie moonlight's view.
Where is my mind?
Traitor must stab behind.
I am writing about how we met,
sometimes the firmament looks violet.
You're like the smell of wet soil,
we must ignore our life's turmoil.
Where is my mind?
Illusion makes us blind.
I am writing about how our story was like a book,
we never took each other for mistook.
The book had to end, with no empty pages,
rat race is so poor when we were trapped into cages.
Where is my mind?
People will be the reason to ruin mankind.
And when I realize maybe the end is sweeter,
after we went out unalterably we cannot reenter.
But then that's not who we were,
we were quite bound to be together.

DEATH OF THE DOVES

The call of birds in the morning sky,
once she stared at me, I felt shy.
sky was dark, with toxic smoke,
bombs were dropping like thunderstroke.

People were running like helpless rats,
blood drunk by the Vampire bats.
her eyes flickered, as if she was leaving,
we cannot skip our fate by skiving.

Dark sky has taken the white doves,
we all have lost our loved ones.
it was the pain of someone's bereaved,
or the mischievous act of someone we believed.

Black rain was falling from the above sky,
the dead doves won't again fly.
I lost her familiar hand,
as if the corpses have been buried in the sand.

When the dragon's wings flied like cottons,
I saw her eyes, like the black buttons.
tears vanished like Camphor,
we made our anaphor,
we got a rendezvous that was long away from arena,
war is always grievous, her name was Serena.

ALLY, WILL SEE YOU

The time since I have known you,
me always being in solitude.
You came like an anonymous,
my feelings saved in multitude.
I saw you many nights in my world, imaginary,
all words are not in my dictionary.
My all wishes for you, are only in my fantasy,
that cannot happen in reality,
if that happens I'll find a wonderful ecstasy,
cause some feelings are for an eternity.
I do not know the definition of love,
we all are like white dove.
Many rainy days I thought of you,
you grimly waved at me,
like I'm near a seashore,
with a breeze that blew against me.
I came near to hate you almost,
I couldn't do that cause of my love, utmost.
My dreams on you are healthy,
like microbes, filthy.
You taught me lessons that cannot be found in a book,
I want to learn more from you,
just don't impend me by a hook.

I always have my interest in cases of curiosity,
you are not in my fortune, that's why I feel anxiety.
You are precious to me ally,
sometimes I feel like a dustbin full of sully.
I cannot dissuade you, I don't want to lose you,
I got you abruptly, will want to embrace you.

LIKE MAGGOTS ON A CORPSE

See the empty space growing beneath the underworld,
that terrible sore, the bloodshot eyes are looking at you.
God's blessing protect the innocents,
he has no food, he does not know what he is doing.
Like Maggots on a Corpse.
The crematorium is filled up with bodies,
the night in the cemetery,
a foul odor next to the sewer,
unscrupulous people are giggling,
some people are megalomaniac towards themselves,
wrongdoers are impugning, meting pseudo propaganda.
Like inserting 'sooth' into the illusion,
fuzzy like morning mist, dim as the eclipsing sun,
just a candle in a darkness.
Despite having eyes, you are running like a blind man.
Regardless we are losing ourselves,
still trying not to stumble.
Waiting for the dawn,
I heard eavesdropping,
"Empire of the Sun".

A VERY FAMILIAR ME

Every now and then you have days, bathed in sunlight,
when the sky says, "it is a brand new day,
Wake up from your sleep and check it."
Why do I love it so much?
I cannot really say,
and somehow I can find myself again.
A very familiar me.
Winds of change,
turn my every day routine upside down,
desire springs up inside me,
what happens to all the rules and regulations?
Why do I love it so much?
I cannot really say,
and somehow I can find myself again.
A very familiar me.
In the process of growing up,
when did life disappear so quickly?
With all the childishness, and random playfulness,
Why do I love it so much?
I cannot really say
and somehow I can find myself again.
A very familiar me.

BETWIXT THE ANATHEMAS

Expectations when flying off the air,
critics do not take it fair.
If that writing creates a social mystery,
perhaps it has to deal with History.
This is a comedy film, an Allegory,
showing the bigotry, so many zealots.
Pseudo patriots are screaming,
Why the soil above the Spine?
The message reaches on its altitude,
rip out the Masquerade, faces of multitude.
Strength of a pen enriches on its nib,
hush again and a certain Manifesto.
An irrefutable truth, molds by violence,
so many cases, Indecisive.
Vintage conception, sour grapes,
in an equilibrium, structure becomes shackles.
The film full with content,
the writing is bombing.
Truth is forever a Taboo,
Propagandas dealing with Forbidding.

www.ingramcontent.com/pod-product-compliance
Lightning Source LLC
LaVergne TN
LVHW041306150826
845673LV00008B/2751

* 9 7 8 9 3 9 1 4 3 1 0 1 3 *